Gallery Books
Editor: Peter Fallon

PILLOW TALK

Paula Meehan

PILLOW TALK

Gallery Books

Pillow Talk
was first published
simultaneously in paperback
and in a clothbound edition
on 22 July 1994.
Reprinted 1997

The Gallery Press
Loughcrew
Oldcastle
County Meath
Ireland

ISBN 1 85235 133 0 (*paperback*)
       1 85235 134 9 (*clothbound*)

The Gallery Press receives financial assistance from An Chomhairle
Ealaíon / The Arts Council, Ireland.

Contents

for Nora Harkin

My Father Perceived as a Vision of St Francis

for Brendan Kennelly

It was the piebald horse in next door's garden
frightened me out of a dream
with her dawn whinny. I was back
in the boxroom of the house,
my brother's room now,
full of ties and sweaters and secrets.
Bottles chinked on the doorstep,
the first bus pulled up to the stop.
The rest of the house slept

except for my father. I heard
him rake the ash from the grate,
plug in the kettle, hum a snatch of a tune.
Then he unlocked the back door
and stepped out into the garden.

Autumn was nearly done, the first frost
whitened the slates of the estate.
He was older than I had reckoned,
his hair completely silver,
and for the first time I saw the stoop
of his shoulder, saw that
his leg was stiff. What's he at?
So early and still stars in the west?

They came then: birds
of every size, shape, colour; they came
from the hedges and shrubs,
from eaves and garden sheds,
from the industrial estate, outlying fields,
from Dubber Cross they came
and the ditches of the North Road.

The garden was a pandemonium
when my father threw up his hands
and tossed the crumbs to the air. The sun

cleared O'Reilly's chimney
and he was suddenly radiant,
a perfect vision of St Francis,
made whole, made young again,
in a Finglas garden.

Handmaid

Lord, when I walked with you under the stars
and we were overcome by desire
and we lay down in the desert night,
I fell into your eyes, tasted your salt.

And, Lord, when I was impaled on you,
gazed on your face with devotion,
you spoke of the hard day's ride
and distances you had crossed to couple with me.

I have opened wide as a rivermouth to you
and would have you invade my cells,
my womb, my heart, my head, O Lordy
do with me what you will.

A Child's Map of Dublin

I wanted to find you Connolly's Starry Plough,
the flag I have lived under since birth or since
I first scanned nightskies and learned the nature of work.
'That hasn't been on show in years,' the porter told us.
They're revising at the National Museum,
all hammers and drills and dust, converting to
an interpretive centre in the usual contemporary style.

The Natural History Museum: found poem
of oriole, kingfisher, sparrowhawk, nightjar,
but the gull drew me strongest — childhood guide
to the freedom and ecstasy of flight. Common
cacophonist, nothing romantic about that squabbler
of windowledges, invader of the one p.m. schoolyard,
wakefollower of sailors. But watch him on a clear ocean

and nothing reads the wind so well. In the updraught
of a sudden love, I walk the northside streets
that whelped me; not a brick remains
of the tenement I reached the age of reason in. Whole
streets are remade, the cranes erect over Eurocrat schemes
down the docks. There is nothing
to show you there, not a trace of a girl

in ankle socks and hand-me-downs, sulking
on a granite step when she can't raise the price of a film,
or a bus to the beach. The movie she ran in her head?
Africa — hostage slave to some Berber prince or, chainmailed,
she is heroine of a hopeless war
spurring her men to death, but honourable death.

Better I take you up Cumberland Street Saturday.
We'll hoke out something foreign and erotic,
from the mounds of cast-offs on the path.
And when the market's over we'll wander home,

only go the streets that are our fancy.
You'll ask me no questions. I'll tell you no lies.

Climb in here between the sheets
in the last light of this April evening. We'll trust
the charts of our bodies. They've brought us
safe to each other, battle-scarred and frayed
at the folds, they'll guide us to many wonders.
Come, let's play in the backstreets and tidal flats
till we fall off the edge of the known world,

and drown.

One Evening in May

The sultry lead and pewter sky
opened on blue immensity
which hung a moment,
then sultry lead and pewter sky

clanged back. I thought I was wise
till I heard her voice; thought
I had the art of mirror plumbing
perfected. Then she showed me

in a blue clearing of clouds
how space can enrapture a mortal.
That small glimpse was worth
all the age's talk in the academies.

Since, I have wandered in a daze
imagining her everywhere, even
in the faces of the sick and damaged.
It's just her style to trick about

shapechanging all the while.
Whatever happens now, I'll be bound
to her rule for life. I pray I'll not rue
the day she parted clouds,

revealed her starry body, her great
snakeshead, her myriad children
feasting at her breasts. She spoke. She said,
'You're mine. Come. Do my bidding.'

The Standing Army

Now that I carry my mother's spear,
wear my sister's gold ring in my ear,
I walk into the future, proud
to be ranked in the warrior caste,
come to play my part in defence
of my people, from my bed of wisdom sprung
to converse with the poets who
even now are flocking in the streets,
eyes aflame, weary of metrical talk,
starved of chant, craving tribal songs.

May Day 1990

The Other Woman

That night when you entered her for the first time
she was the lonely city, and you were a man with a key
to a room in a house on a street where you might go out of the
    rain
and sit by the window to drink lemon vodka

with no tales to tell, no questions, no answers, no
hope of tomorrow. Not silence; but breath and the fall
of rain to the garden. No light but streetlight.
She was in shadow. You were a stranger and all

she could trust was what she read of your path
when you held out your hand and said come.
She was scribed on your fateline, her own name there
was a song half-remembered, hot on your tongue,

hot on the white sheets you tangled your selves up in.
They were your sails and she was the port in every girl
you knew you were born free for; and bound
to the rule of the sea, her grief, her pulse, her moody

river, her sulky moons, the way they hid for months
under cloud, you were humble. I understood all this
when she woke the next morning to rain on the city.
For my work I need starlight preferably

and plenty of time on my hands. I made her dream
sunshine, a tower, a golden fish atop it, a street
running down to a harbour, a ship just docked,
a stranger approaching with the key to her door.

City

1 *Hearth*

What is the fire you draw to
when you clutch each other
between the sheets? What cold do
you fear? What drives you near
madness, the jealousy you daily
bear? That tyrant time
sifting through the glass? Tell me
a story, not in rhyme
or made up fancy but plain
as the ash in the grate.
The windowpane rattles, the rain
beats about the house. Late
drinkers are turfed from the bar. Wind
snatches their song, tosses it down-
river to the sea pulsing in your mind.
You slip your moorings, cruise the town.

2 Night Walk

Out here you can breathe.
Between showers, the street
empty. Forget your lover
faithless in the chilly bed
who'll wake soon and wonder
if you've left for good.
Granite under your feet
glitters, nearby a siren. Threat

or a promise? You take Fumbally Lane
to the Blackpitts, cut back by the canal.
Hardly a sound you've made, creature
of night in grey jeans and desert boots,
familiar of shade. Listen.
                          The train
bearing chemicals to Mayo, a dog far off, the fall
of petals to the paths of the Square,
a child screaming in a third floor flat.

On Mount Street high heels clack,
stumble in their rhythm, resume.
Let her too get home safe, your prayer,
not like that poor woman last night
dragged down Glovers Alley, raped there,
battered to a pulp. Still unnamed.
Your key in the door, you've made it back,
a chorus of birds predicting light.

3 *Man Sleeping*

How deep are you, how far under?
Here's rosemary I stole on my walk
and the first lilac from the Square.
I lay them on the quilt. You talk
in your dreaming. *I am the beating tide,*
mine is the shore. Taste of the sea,
pulse of my heart. *Don't leave me,*
don't leave me. I dive beneath
and you stiffen to my mouth.
You'll be deep within me when you wake,
your pulse my own. Wave that I ride,
I'll take everything before you break.

4 *Full Moon*

She's up there. You'd know the pull,
stretching you tight as a drumhead,
anywhere. This morning lull
between the alarm and quitting the bed
you consider the scrawb on his back —
sigil of grief: the thumbscrew, the rack.
A paleskin staked on the desert floor
bound at ankle, at neck, at wrist,
no cavalry in sight to even the score.
This is the knife in the gut; this is its twist.

She's up there. Tonight they'll dish out
more downers in prison, in the mental
asylum, tonight there'll be more blood spilt
on the street, and you will howl
to her through the tattered cloud scrawled
across the windowpane, a howl fated
by the blemish on his shoulderblade.
Ask yourself: *To what shapechanger has he mated?*

5 *On the Warpath*

The full moon is drawing you tight
as a drumhead. Your face in the mirror
is cloudy, overcast. No sunny spells;
frost inland tonight.

Reconnoitre the terrain of the heart,
scan for high ground. Ambush, skirmish,
reprisal, this deadly game you play
give as good as you get.

Choose protective colouring, camouflage,
know your foe, every move of him,
every bar of his battle hymn.
Though the outward face is dead cas-

ual, within the self is coiled:
unsprung, the human, suddenly, wild.

Not Your Muse

I'm not your muse, not that creature
in the painting, with the beautiful body,
Venus on the half-shell. Can
you not see I'm an ordinary woman
tied to the moon's phases, bloody
six days in twenty-eight? Sure

I'd like to leave you in love's blindness,
cherish the comfort of your art, the way
it makes me whole and shining,
smooths the kinks of my habitual distress,
never mentions how I stumble into the day,
fucked up, penniless, on the verge of whining

at my lot. You'd have got away with it
once. In my twenties I often traded a bit
of sex for immortality. That's a joke.
Another line I swallowed, hook
and sinker. Look at you —
rapt, besotted. Not a gesture that's true

on that canvas, not a droopy breast,
wrinkle or stretchmark in sight.
But if it keeps you happy who am I
to charge in battledressed to force you test
your painted doll against the harsh light
I live by, against a brutal merciless sky.

Good Friday, 1991

The low tide reveals him
tangled in plastic and branches
snagged at the foot of Capel Street bridge.

How he came to be there,
whether he jumped off
the quay wall or slipped
quietly into the green water,
another city mystery.
                              And what
of the children watching?
The fire brigade, the grappling hooks,
the boat inching up the shallows;
what of the soul manhandling
the body over the stern
who looks up suddenly to our staring faces?

Though we glimpsed his face
but briefly, it's there before me now
white as the snow of Komarovo,
his slender drenched body
that no arms can succour,
his song and pattern ended
under the fast spring clouds,
a strong wind from the east
ruffling the low Liffey waters.

Laburnum

You walk into an ordinary room
on an ordinary evening, say
mid May, when the laburnum

hangs over the railings of the Square
and the city is lulled by eight o'clock,
the traffic sparse, the air fresher.

You expect to find someone
waiting, though now you live
alone. You've answered none

of your calls. The letters pile
up in the corner. The idea
persists that someone waits while

you turn the brass handle and knock
on the light. Gradually
the dark seeps into the room, you lock

out the night, scan a few books.
It's days since you ate.
The plants are dying — even the cactus,

shrivelled like an old scrotum,
has given up the ghost. There's
a heel of wine in a magnum

you bought, when? The day
before? The day before that?
It's the only way

out. The cold sweats
begin. You knock back a few.
You've no clean clothes left.

He is gone. Say it.
Say it to yourself, to the room.
Say it loud enough to believe it.

You will live breath
by breath. The beat of your own heart
will scourge you. You'll wait

in vain, for he's gone from you.
And every night is a long
slide to the dawn you

wake to, terrified in your ordinary room
on an ordinary morning, say
mid May, say the time of laburnum.

Playing House

You have prepared a room for me,
a desk below a high window
giving on coachhouses, lanes,
a wild garden of elder and ash.

Home, you say, let this be
a home for you. Unpack
your clothes, hang them
beside mine. Put your sharp
knife in my kitchen, your books
in my stacks. Let your face
share my mirrors. Light
fires in my hearth. Your talismans
are welcome. Break bread
with me. Settle. Settle.

'When you left the city you carried . . .'

When you left the city you carried
off the May sun, left heavy skies.
A bad spell was cast on the island:
colour leached from blossom, birds fell mute,
the Liffey stopped dreaming of the sea,
the eyes of the citizenry grew frosty
and for two weeks now I have moved
like a zombie through my life.
All I turn my hand to
snags. I can't sleep nights. I fret,
demented with desire for your body
weaving in sea motion under mine.
Close to dawn I hit the streets
and walk in hope of losing you,
in hope of peace. Christ I'd give
ten years of my span to look on your face
for an instant, to fall into your eyes
that are the sea blue of desert mornings,
to dive through the fiery coronas,
drown in the depths of your pupils.
Days are spent in superstitious rite:
penny candles at Valentine's shrine,
invocations to an Eastern goddess
to please watch over your journey,
to bring you home safe,
and if anyone should lay a finger on you
or harm a hair of your head
there'll be no hiding from my wrath
on this, or any other, planet.

Night Prayer

                        So far
from me tonight across the city
beyond the huddled terraces of brick,
past the prison, the hospital on call,
through the markets, the shopping malls,
over the river, the fashionable streets
and the back lanes, past the Dáil,
the Museum, the Library, the Gallery:
your house on the Square where laburnum flowers
fall.
            I will my self to fly
through the sheets of rain. I am
the sudden squall at your blinds. Hear me.

Go to your window, look out —
the moon is safe above the clouds
growing as our child grows in me
safely, a secret still.
                                I inhabit
the rain. Lean out. I'll wash
over your body, cleanse you of burdens
you've carried too long, rinse you of grief
and ghosts of old that batter your heart.
Away with them. I wish you
a clear day to walk in, no fear, no shame,
a day of rain falling,
a day of rain ceasing,
yourself with a calm heart
walking into the day
to possess it entirely,
your mind free of riddles and scourging confusions.

Let you have one day such as I'd make
for you, a clear day to dream and shape,
a day of waves beating,

of song whorling within,
so you may bequeath it long years after
to your son or your daughter, whichever
I bear you.

Pillow Talk

These hot midsummer nights I whisper
assignations, trysts, heather beds
I'd like to lay you down in, remote beaches
we could escape to, watch
bonfire sparks mix with stars.
I want you to stay alive till we two
meet again, to hold the line, to ignore
the gossip traded about me in the marketplace.
I fall back on cliché, the small
change of an adulterous summer,
plots of half-hatched movies, theories
of forked lightning, how you make
the soles of my feet burn when I come.

What you don't hear is the other voice
when she speaks through me
beyond human pity or mercy. She wants you.
Put her eye on you the first time
she saw you. And I'm powerless,
a slave to her whim. She shall
have you. What can I do
when she speaks of white river stones,
elfin grots, her sacred birds?
I know she once tore a man apart,
limb from limb with her bare hands
in some rite in her bloody past.
My stomach turns at the hot
relentless stench of her history.

Nights you stare out
panic-stricken through the mask,
I think you may have heard her speak:
you realize that you ride a demon,
that the dark has no end to it.

Though I mean you no grief,
I cannot vouchsafe her intent. I fear
not all my healing arts can salve
the wound she has in store for you.

Silk

You dance in a length of shiny silk
lately acquired in a Tashkent bazaar,
charming me with every slink
of your hips, teeth aflash.

Haven't we met somewhere
before — by a gypsy fire
or in a blue domed marketplace
where slaves are traded for new gold?

If you seek to bind me
this summer with sex and cool melon,
don't bother. I'm already bound
and lost and falling fast,

tumbling head over heels
down the abyss.
                    To think
I've waited centuries for this!
You dancing in shiny silk

in the afternoon, stealing an hour
from work. And where
does it end?
                    Work and love:
the heart's hunger, the daily bread.

Breagaim Breagaim Breagaim
I woo I lie I woo
and if you walk away from me
on a hot city street

I'll not look after you.
But turn
into my own mystery. Though
it may take centuries to find you again,
dancing wantonly in silk.

Aubade

after an image by Joan Miró

And then we dress for the June sun.
You hand me a small bird to guard me,
to make a song only I can hear.
We part on the corner; I spin
like a top through the city,
through the hot streets.
Nothing can harm me.
Nothing disturb me.
Not all the tantric fruit on Moore Street,
the beggar's cupped hand,
the grey-suited ones,
the kept ladies of the rich,
the men with rape in their hearts,
the dole queue blues,
the priest sweating in black,
the sleazy deals of our rulers,
the prisoner in her pox hole of a cell,
the warder and her grating keys,
the embalmer's curious art,
the thunderbolts of a Catholic god,
the useless tears of His mother.
You've given me a small bird
to guard me, to sing me spinning songs,
the gift of our journey
and a safe place to rest in.
I stand in that centre,
the still place you grant me,
just like any other woman
with a bird in front of the sun.

'Would you jump into my grave as quick?'

Would you jump into my grave as quick?
my granny would ask when one of us took
her chair by the fire. You, woman,
done up to the nines, red lips a come on,
your breath reeking of drink
and your black eye on my man tonight
in a Dublin bar, think
first of the steep drop, the six dark feet.

The Ghost of My Mother Comforts Me

after Van Morrison

Do not fear, daughter,
when they lift their sticks, their stones,
when they hiss beneath their breaths —

*Fallen woman, adulteress, breaker of marriage vows
made before a holy priest to an honourable man.*

For you, daughter, there is no blame,
for you no portion of guilt,
for you're made in my likeness.
You can take the crucifixion from your voice.
I will stroke your forehead till you sleep,
till you pass over into the dreamworld
where we can walk together in gardens wet with rain
or fly along old star roads
or sit quietly near running water.

And when you wake refreshed
you'll be ready for their sticks, their stones,
their names that cannot hurt you.
Balance your gypsy soul, lodged
in the body given you, my daughter,
for your pleasure and as a tool for struggle,
against the weight of the world's troubles.
Take comfort in the knowledge that you are not alone.
There are many like you on the earth,
and you will be numbered among the warriors
when the great book is written.

Because I am your mother I will protect you
as I promised you in childhood.
You will walk freely on the planet,

my beloved daughter. Fear not
the lightning bolts of a Catholic god, or any other,
for I have placed my body and my soul between you
   and all harm.

Autobiography

She stalks me through the yellow flags.
If I look over my shoulder I will catch her
striding proud, a spear in her hand.
I have such a desperate need of her —
though her courage springs
from innocence or ignorance. I could lie with her
in the shade of the poplars, curled
to a foetal dream on her lap, suck
from her milk of fire to enable me fly.
Her face is my own face unblemished;
her eyes seapools, reflecting lichen,
thundercloud; her pelt like watered silk
is golden. She guides me to healing herbs
at meadow edges. She does not speak
in any tongue I recognize.
She is mother to me, young
enough to be my daughter.

The other one waits in gloomy hedges.
She pounces at night. She knows I've no choice.
She says: 'I am your future.
Look on my neck, like a chicken's
too old for the pot; my skin moults
in papery flakes. Hear it rustle?
My eyes are the gaping wounds
of newly opened graves. Don't turn
your nose up at me, madam.
You may have need of me yet.
I am your ticket underground.' And yes
she has been suckled at my own breast.
I breathed deep of the stench of her self —
the stink of railway station urinals,
of closing-time vomit, of soup lines
and charity shops. She speaks
in a human voice and I understand.

I am mother to her, young
enough to be her daughter.

I stand in a hayfield — midday, midsummer,
my birthday. From one breast
flows the Milky Way, the starry path,
a sluggish trickle of pus from the other.
When I fly off I'll glance back
once, to see my husk sink into the grasses.
Cranesbill and loosestrife will shed
seeds over it like a blessing.

'Not alone the rue in my herb garden . . . '

Not alone the rue in my herb garden
passes judgement, but the eight foot
high white foxgloves among the greys
of wormwood, santolina, lavender,
the crimson rose at our cottage door,
the peas holding for dear life to their sticks
and the smaller drowning salad stuff.
The weeds grow lush and lovely
at midsummer, honeysuckle roving
through the hawthorn: my garden
at Eslin ferociously passing judgement.

We built this soil together, husband;
barrow after barrow load of peat
sieved through an old chip strainer
and the heaps of rotted manure
pushed over frosty paths on still
midwinter days, or when an east wind
chewed at our knuckles. Cranky
of a morning when the range acted up,
we still saved wood ash and dug it in,
by Christmas laid a mulch of hay
and tucked it all up safe in beds,
turned off the light and spent the most
of January and February, the bitterest days,
at chess, or poem and story making.

You were beautiful in my father's
ravelled jumper, staring at the rain,
or painting revelations of the hag
that scared the living daylights out of me.
One canvas was blacker than
the lower pits of hell after an eternity
when even the scourging fire has gone out
and the tortured souls are silenced.

O heart of my husband, I thought,
how little have I fathomed thee,
when you went and overpainted it
on a St Brigid's Day of snow and crocuses,
with a green-eyed young fiddler,
named it *Mystery Dame with Red Hair*.

We built this garden together, husband;
germinated seeds in early spring,
gambling with a crystal dice,
moon calendars and almanacs,
risked seedlings to a late black frost,
wept at loss — but some survived
to thrive a summer of aching backs.
A festive air when the poles went up
and scarlet runners coiled along the twine.
Mornings I walked out after a shower

had tamped the dust and turned
the volume way up on birdsong,
on scent, on colour, I counted myself
the luckiest woman born, to gain such
an inland kingdom, three wild
rushy acres, edged by the Eslin
trickily looping us below the hill,
our bass line to the Shannon
and the fatal rhythm of the Atlantic swell.

I did not cast it off lightly,
the yoke of work, the years of healing,
of burying my troubled dead
with every seed committed to the earth,
judging their singular, particular needs,
nurturing them with sweat and prayer
to let the ghosts go finally from me

with every basket of the harvest
I garnered in golden light for our table,
something singing in me all the while,
a song of fate, of fortune, of a journey,
a twisty road that led away from you,
my husband of the sea-scarred eyes.

Now that I return to visit you,
abandoned gardens, abandoned husband,
abandoned cat and dog and chickens,
abandoned quilts and embroideries,
high piled books, my dusty drafts,
a life I stitched together out of love,
and we sit together by the window
in the summer light, the sculptural
clouds of June, their whimsical shadows
oblivious of the grief on our faces,
in sorrow at what we built and lost
and never will rebuild, O my friend,
do not turn on me in hatred,
do not curse the day we met.

Berlin Diary, 1991

1 *At the Pergamon*

The swastika at the centre
of the terracotta plate
behind security glass
in the Pergamon Museum
looks so wholly innocent.
I try to imagine the day of the potter,
a Sumerian day in 230 BC
by the bank of the Euphrates perhaps,
the clay centring on the wheel,
the thumb brought to bear
still there in the fine ridging
at the rim. This plate —
balance of held and holding,
the cold air of the museum,
the hum of the air conditioning,
the drone of a tour guide,
and the boots, the boots, the boots
of the guard echoing. My head
begins to spin.
          The plate
begins to spin. Swastika!
Black spinning sun of my own black pupil
thrown back from the glass. My eye
and swastika one
              black spinning sun!

2 *On Being Taken for a Turkish Woman*

I did not plan it but the clothes I chose that morning for the damp day that's in it — long navy overcoat, grey silk headscarf, and in my left ear a blue stone — makes me look like a Turkish woman.

And I am bound for the Turkish market at Kreuzberg. On the U-Bahn and the S-Bahn and the trams, so many graffiti swastikas my eyes are aching. I break my journey at Rosa Luxembourg Platz because I like the name.

A man up a ladder is postering over a street sign: Carrot Street. Carrot Street? I ask why. *All names Communist gone with the Wall.* There will be Cabbage Street and Turnip Street and Rutabaga Street and Gherkin Street.

I have no gift to bring home to my friend, and the mist is thickening and night coming on. I come to a U-Bahn. I ask directions to Kreuzberg. The man behind the counter nearly spits in my face. Misdirects me. I've a three mile walk along the canal: the lindens, the odd citizen walking a dog, a gang of mean looking youths, all looming out of the mist.

I am considering the nature of betrayal and the circumstances in an Izmir bazaar, his eye suddenly caught by the blue luminescence of the stone that now adorns my left ear. *The sign of one who's chosen the path of the warrior rather than the path of the lover*, he said when he gave it to me.

I'm trying to work all this out in iambic, trying to find the strong steady pulse of my walkabout in words. But there's too much danger at the edges, and I need all my concentration for reading the street. Visibility is down to a few yards and I've no way of knowing what will come at me next out of the mist. Another gang could materialize; or the same gang from twenty minutes ago could be coming back to get me having only now processed the signals of my garb.

When my friend gave me the earring he said it reminded him of the Miraculous Medal his mother used pin on his gansy when he was a boy, and followed it with a long rigmarole on Mariology, Earth goddesses, the power of the female, mid-Eastern moon worship, blue as a healing colour, as Mary's colour.

When I finally find the market they are packing up their wares. I choose a jet and gold anklet. I pay the jewel hawker the marks I owe her and she wraps it up. A blue stone glitters at her throat, another on her baby's blanket. *Good luck*, she says, *and health to wear it*.

3 *Handmade*

Your manifesto on my body
the yellow bruise on my breast
the exact same colour as the willow
at my window on Majakowskiring.

4 *A Different Eden*

The morning I left Dublin you were telling me a story —
a suppressed genesis. How Lilith
who pre-dated Eve went about the garden
and asked each creature, each plant,
to tell her its original name.
I pictured her stooped to a mandrake. *Mandragora
    Officianarum.*
What the plant said to her,
or she to it for that matter, is a mystery.

We call things by their given names
as I imagine Adam meant for us to do
strutting round the garden —
You Giraffe! Me God'sman! and poor
spare-ribbed Eve tempted
by the snake totem of her wiser sister
gets them shagged into the wilderness.

5 *Folktale*

A young man falls in love with Truth and searches the wide world for her. He finds her in a small house, in a clearing, in a forest. She is old and stooped. He swears himself to her service — to chop wood, to carry water, to collect the root, the stem, the leaf, the flowering top, the seed of each plant she needs for her work.

Years go by. One day the young man wakes up longing for a child. He goes to the old woman and asks to be released from his oath so that he may return to the world. *Certainly*, she says, *but on one condition: you must tell them that I am young and that I am beautiful.*

6 *What I Saw on Stargartenstrasse*

Smokestack, shunting train,
cobbles scored where
her high heels have graven
ghost music in the mist.
I'm searching for my mother
after another war.

She was broody, like Sophie,
a golden hen in a story she'd tell me
to keep the nightmares away.

Ghost music on Stargartenstrasse
her high heels fragmenting cobbles,
my golden broody hen.

Oak leaves trodden to dust,
the army marches past
smokestack, shunting train.
We'll not pass this way again.

7 At Pankow S-Bahn

I remember this episode. A German friend, a native of Berlin, has come to visit me on Papa Stour, a small island in the Shetland Islands. The first time he needs a shit, I give him a shovel and tell him to walk to the wild side of the island. From then on he calls the place *The Shitlands*. Close to the end of his stay we are sitting by the range after a long day gathering fuel. It's been hard work; mostly retrieving pine poles from a deep cove — no path down, straight over the cliff on a rope — but a good haul to be traded for coal or burnt itself. A fortnight's heat, a fortnight's writing and hot water worth of pine. It's two in the morning. There's the dusky light of this far northern midsummer, the *simmer dim* as the people around call it. He's picking out a tune on my Epiphone, humming. It's a Dylan song — *when you got nothing, you got nothing to lose*. I'm working through a basket of mending. I'm pleased with a patch on my jeans, the tricky way I have found to set it in, following the contours of my own ass. Neat. I embroider a small *Om* in white silk for luck on the crotch, though any man now would reach a *vagina dentata* rather than *The Gates of Awe*. He asks me to mend his waistcoat, a tear, *a couple of stitches would do it, it was my grandfather's*. I estimate. Two hours work. A darning job on the heavy worsted; and a finicky delicate stitching needed for the lining. Silk? A button gone. Have I a match? What's this? In the candlelight I make out the raised pattern on the remaining buttons. *Swastikas? Was your grandfather a Nazi?* Blurted out into what becomes a moment's terror — a look of pure hatred. I cannot unpick those words.

I fix the waistcoat carefully. You would have to look hard to find the mending. I strengthen some seams and sponge away the shiny grime at the neck, drape it above the range. If I hold anything of that day forever it will be his face staring down at me over the cliff's edge as he feeds out the rope with great care and concentration, my life in his hands.

The Russian Doll

Her colours caught my eye.
Mixed by the light of a far off sun:
carmine, turmeric, indigo, purple —
they promised to spell us dry weather.

I'd a fiver in my pocket; that's
all they asked for. And gift wrapped her.
It had been grey all month and damp.
We felt every year in our bones

and our dead had been too much with us.
January almost over. Bitter.
I carried her home like a Holy Fire
the seven miles from the town,

my face to a wind from the north. Saw
the first primroses in the maw of a fallen oak.
There was smoke from the chimney
when I came through the woods

and, though I had spent the dinner,
I knew you'd love your gaudy doll,
you'd love what's in her
at the end of your seventh winter.

The Wounded Child

1

First — gird yourself. Put on
a talisman. It may be precious
metal or common stone.

What matters is you believe
it powerful, ensurer of
a protective zone to ward off evil,

what matters is *baraka*
from years of kindly use; or that it be
a token of a good time, like a

night under a lucky star,
untroubled, with a gentle man
who means you no harm,

or a ring given in friendship —
a calm room, maybe spring,
the light spinning out, you sip

tea and talk long into darkness
of old lives and dreamtimes,
journeys that brought you near bliss.

2

Whatever you wear you'll be strange.
This is battledress. Paint your face,
put feathers in your hair, arrange
your skirts, your skins, your lace.

Your own eyes stare out clear,
unfazed, from the bedroom mirror.
Though the mask is not familiar
your own eyes stare out. With no fear.

You are able for this.

3

Somewhere in the girl you once were
is the wounded child. Find her.
You have to find her.

She is lonely. Terrified. Curled
to a foetal grip in a tight place,
sobbing her heart out. The world

is a man with big hands
and sharp teeth. The world
is a ton of bricks, sand

in her mouth, a huge weight
on her chest. She has no breath
to speak of it. Her fate

is unwritten, silent, mute.
Remember her? Remember
her splitting apart. Tell her truth.

4

Pick her up. *Go on!*
Hold her close to you.
Hold her to your breast.
If you cannot find the words
at first, hum the tune.
They will come eventually;
like a spell or a prayer
they are already there.

When she has quietened
tell her the story of the Russian doll:

A child, lost in a forest, curls in the lip of a fallen birch
among fern and moss. She sleeps. Dreams of her mother.
She clutches a wooden doll. The woodcutter draws near.
She hears beat of axe, saw's clean song. Freed of bole, of
branches, the stump swings back, closes over her like a
great mouth. And still she dreams, opening doll after
doll, seeking the kernel carved from birch heartwood,
seeking the smallest doll she can hold in her palm. Fire
consumes the forest; smoke obscures the sun. Deer and
wolf alike flee the hungry tongues. A birch seedling
thrives on the spot, thrives through the seasons until it is
the finest sapling in the forest. The girl pushes through
rings, sheds silver bark on the snow. The yellow years
fall, ripple out forever. Passing, you might hear her voice
and name it *Wind-in-Leaves*. Your heart would ache with
loneliness. She dreams of nut within shell, scrolls back to
birth of glacier, forward to death of sun. The woodcutter
finds her pliant to the whim of the wind. She surrenders
to beat of axe, to saw's clean song, welcomes the familiar
refrain.

5

When your story is told
give her the Russian doll.
Make her peel away layer after layer
till she gains the inmost figure
from the birch's heartwood whittled
so small the face has lost its human guise.
Say: *Take this in your fist, love,*
grip tight and feel
glacier grind mountain to dust,
fire gallop across the taiga,
sunlight pulse through your leaves,
snow melt to nourish your roots;
bend with grace before the wind's might,
embrace beat of axe, saw's clean song.

Rescue the child
                    from her dark spell!
Rescue the child
                    from her dark spell!
Rescue the child.

25 February 1992

She-Who-Walks-Among-The-People

'Tell me a story, Granny. Not the one
about the little girl lost in the forest,
not the one about the grandmother who turns
into a big wolf and eats the little girl up.
Do you remember *that* one, Granny? The wolf's
teeth dripping with the little girl's blood?
Tell me the story about the kind lady
who became a great warrior in the old days.'

'Child of grace, look into the flames.
Long, long ago, not in my granny's time,
nor in her granny's before her, but further back
in a world you couldn't imagine, a bad spell
was cast on the whole island. The people lived
in fear and pain. The land itself was hurting,
as were the animals who shared it with the people.
One tribe fought against the next tribe
and at night their dreams were muddy and grey.
One tribe had many, many tokens
and owned all the land and chariots and most
of the things on the island. Another tribe
had some tokens, just enough for food and shelter.
And some tribes had no tokens at all. None
of them could get any peace or clear dreamings
with the worry about tokens, whether they had
any or not. The tribes who had nothing were
broken in spirit. Nobody cared about them,
and nobody listened to them. A terrible silence
stole over them: words were stones on their tongues.
Their children, charmed by strange potions, bad visions,
grew thin and sickened and faded away to death.
Or turned with the tide from the shores to carry
their learning and vigour like makeshift bundles
to the doors of strangers. Some went mad,
the burden of silence too heavy on their shoulders,

and were locked away in dungeons. They could make
no sense of a world that shifted them to
high towers or dumped them in huge encampments
with no tokens, no hope, no dreams for a future.
A little girl like you wouldn't be safe walking
in the world for there were many damaged people
who had turned into monsters and forgotten
the human way. They were as sharks in the streets
of the city, ravening wolves in the countryside.

And the silence was heavy on the island
like a mourning shroud; lies were thick
on the tongues of the rulers. Few were the lawgivers
who cared about justice, few were the doctors
who cared about healing, few were the teachers
who cared about truth. But some there were
and they were as shining warriors among the people.
And one in special who came from the Northwest,
near to the site of the Holy Mountain, where
the Great Sea beats the rock to sand under the sun.
The tunes of that place sparkle like salmon curving
upriver to their dark spawning ground. She
was a slip of a girl with laughter in her eyes and just
about your own age when her heart opened
with pity for the people and pity for the women
in special, for back then the women were slaves
and had to do what the men told them to do.
She studied hard at her books and learned
all there was to learn about the Laws,
and she saw that some Laws were cruel, especially
the Laws for the women. She went to the courts
of the island and fought for the women there
with her marvellous gift of speech. When she got
no satisfaction there she went to the big courts
on the mainland. And she was greatly

beloved by the people and they made her chief
among all the warriors. They had begun
to speak again and break the spell of silence.
They laughed at the liars and took away their Powers.
She'd come and stand among the people and listen.
Wherever they organized and struggled she'd be there
to give them courage and bear witness to their
hard work and service. And though her original
name is lost in the mists of Time and Change
we remember her as She-Who-Walks-Among-The-People.
That was the name the poets and song makers
gave her long ago, not in my granny's time, nor
in her granny's before her, but further back
in a world, child of grace, you couldn't imagine.'

'And, Granny, did the people live happy ever after?'

'The people will endure. They are scattered
over the face of the earth like those stars
above you over the face of the heavens.
Our dreams are as clear as water from a good well
and we mind each other. But who knows when
a bad spell will be cast on the island again?
That's why you must work hard at your books,
in case one day you'll be needed by the people.
If you aren't a good girl *you'll* go down in the songs as
Girl-Gobbled-By-A-Wolf-She-Thought-Was-Her-Granny!'

Mrs Sweeney

I cast my song on the water.
The sky stirs,
clouds are driven under the trailing willow.

I cast my song on the water.
The sky in your hungry eye, you drop
to meet the cloud's image.

Your eye most nights is sparrowhawk.
So strike. Flip me over. Pin
my wings with your talons.
Pluck, then, my breast feathers
to the creamy skin over my heart.
Flash of beak as you stoop to pierce.

Island Burial

They bury their dead as quick as they can
before the shapechanging shames them
and gets them branded as witches.
I know a family had to watch their dead daughter
turn into a hare before their eyes.
They coffined her quick but swear
they heard paws against the coffin lid
as they lowered her down, as the clay fell.

1 *Song of the Grave*

I am the grave waiting
patient receptive damp
for my hare girl in flux

when she's entered her hare self
I'll close like a fist
an end to her thumping rut

a long time hence
when you prise open my fingers
her bones on my palm

know I have cherished her

2 *Prayer at the Graveside*

Burying our dead
Flesh to dust
Dust on the wind
Ash on your brow
Song of the yew
Chalice of darkness

3 *How the Children Tell It*

hare field witch
burning hare crack
cloud sea rock
a bye long sleep

hare lope green
path gate stream
sun white stone
belly breath come

hare heron cry
sand grain star
foot before foot
up stony road

hare paws hare
paws beat on wood
hare spent kick
blue eye watch

knife rope cut
home safe feather

Dream Filter

Before you were born,
I made a dream filter
to ensure you clear dreamings

for the whole of your childhood,
to the exact specifications
of a tribe I read about

in *National Geographic*. First
I'd to clear my own dreams
and pass all my bad visions

into stones; then go on foot
to pure swift running water
near where it entered the sea

and cast each weighted stone
to the pebbly bed
where they could be washed to a calm

stonedness again. Only
then was I fit to begin.

              ❧

The finding of coppiced hazel,
the twisting of hempen twine,
the building of the dream filter

itself, took a full seven months.
*Wait for a bird
to gift you some feathers.*

On the walk to the hospital
down by the South Docks,
after a night spent in labour,

three slate-grey feathers there in my path.
I looked up and saw
a peregrine falcon hung in the air —

one of a pair that were nesting
on top of the gasometer.

≈ ≋

This contraption
made of hazel and hemp
and a few tail feathers

is fixed tonight above your cradle.
One day you'll ask
what it's all about.

And what can I tell you?
What can I possibly say?

Birthday Present

When your father came for you
the month you turned four
you were deep in the woods with the goat.

I told him the wolves had carried you off
and left me alone.

His hands made me lie:
his soft white hands,
his short lifeline,
and what I read of his fate.

Blessing

for Tony Curtis

Not to the colony for artists
not to the walled university
but to the demented asylum
I'll go when the moon is up
in the day sky, I'll go

and snatch a song from a stranger's mouth.

They have been speaking so long
in riddles they teach you
the heart for a child breaking,
the heart breaking for a child
is nothing more than a shift
of light on a slate roof
after rain, and the elderberry's
purpling shade is as much
as you'll know of grieving.

They have been speaking so long
in riddles the world believes at last
in enigma, the earth understands
her beguiling work —
        leaf, stone, wave.

To the demented asylum I'll go
for succour from a stranger's mouth:
    leaf crown you
        wave repeat you
            stone secure your grave

'The rain makes one word . . .'

The rain makes one word

for the woman when they quarrel.
It falls on the city.

Her boots let in
but they got her through the winter.

The rain makes one word that drops
in the silence when it stops

and the window weeps
beads — each a convex mirror

of the room where
she's polishing her boots.

Loss: the rain made.
Loss. She stares

at the boots
that have got her through the winter.

Home

I am the blind woman finding her way home by a map of tune.
When the song that is in me is the song I hear from the world
I'll be home. It's not written down and I don't remember the
    words.
I know when I hear it I'll have made it myself. I'll be home.

A version I heard once in Leitrim was close, a wet Tuesday
    night
in the Sean Relig bar. I had come for the session, I stayed
for the vision and lore. The landlord called time,
the music dried up, the grace notes were pitched to the dark.
When the jukebox blared out *I'd only four senses and he left me
    senseless*,
I'd no choice but to take to the road. On Grafton Street in
    November
I heard a mighty sound: a travelling man with a didgeridoo
blew me clear to Botany Bay. The tune too far back to live in
but scribed on my bones. In a past life I may have been
    Kangaroo,
rocked in my dreamtime, convict ships coming o'er the foam.

In the Puzzle Factory one winter I was sure I was home.
The talking in tongues, the riddles, the rhymes, struck a chord
that cut through the pharmaceutical haze. My rhythm
    catatonic,
I lulled myself back to the womb, my mother's heart
beating the drum of herself and her world. I was tricked
by her undersong, just close enough to my own. I took then
to dancing; I spun like a Dervish. I swear I heard the subtle
music of the spheres. It's no place to live, but —
out there in space, on your own, hung aloft the night.
The tune was in truth a mechanical drone;
I was a pitiful monkey jigging on cue. I came back to earth
with a land, to rain on my face, to sun in my hair. And grateful
    too.

The wisewomen say you must live in your skin, call *it* home,
no matter how battered or broken, misused by the world, you
    can heal.
This morning a letter arrived on the nine o'clock post.
The Department of Historical Reparation, and who did I
    blame?
The Nuns? Your Mother? The State? *Tick box provided,*
we'll consider your case. I'm burning my soapbox, I'm taking
the very next train. A citizen of nowhere, nothing to my name.

I'm on my last journey. Though my lines are all wonky
they spell me a map that makes sense. Where the song that is in
    me
is the song I hear from the world, I'll set down my burdens
and sleep. The spot that I lie on at last the place I'll call home

Acknowledgements

Acknowledgements are made to the editors of *Aquarius, At Six O'Clock in the Silence of Things, Éire-Ireland, Exposure* (Omagh Writers' Group), *The Irish Times, Krino, Mná na hEorpa Broadsheet* (International Women's Day 1993), *Mná na hEorpa Pamphlet* (International Women's Day 1992), *The New Triangle* (Mountjoy Women's Writing Group), *The Scarlet Quarterly, Seneca Review, Soho Square, Southern Plains Review, The Steeple, Toward Harmony — a Celebration: for Tony O'Malley, Trinity Poetry Broadsheet, UNDR,* and *Windows Broadsheet* where some of these poems were published; and to Arté TV (France), BBC Northern Ireland, BBC Radio 4, BBC Radio Foyle, Kilkenny Local Radio, RTE Radio 1 ('The Arts Show' and 'Sunday Miscellany'), and Women's Aid, where some were recorded and broadcast.

A version of 'Pillow Talk' accompanied two paintings by Eithne Jordan at The Rubicon Gallery, July 1992.

'The Wounded Child' was the text for a dance performed by Rubato, choreographed by Fiona Quilligan, to a score by Fergus Johnson, Dublin Theatre Festival 1992.

'She-Who-Walks-Among-The-People' was commissioned by Combat Poverty Agency to honour President Mary Robinson and presented to her on 19 April 1993.